# This book would not have been possible without the generous support of these people

## Team Renfrow Super Star

Gail J. Bonath
Anne F. Harris
Russelle Jones Leggett
Deidre McLay
Maribeth McLay
Paula Nixon
Joan "Dusty" Ohnemus

## Team Renfrow Gold Star

Karna Smith Bosman
Lynn Cavanagh
Darwin & Jeanette Copeman
Jerry & Carolyn Grosenbach
Jan & Dan Gross
Gregg & Diane Hawkins
Judy Hunter
Jill & Dan Kaiser
Sue Kolbe
Catherine Rod
Tanya Smith & Jim Tipton

## Team Renfrow

Jill Allen
Barbara Ashby
Sheryl Bissen
Suzanne & Lowell Bunger
Kate, Allen, Parm & Rory Chan
Sue Ratcliff Drake
David Ferguson
Debbie Gottschalk
Allison Haack
Valerie Hammond
Ann R. Igoe
April Van Ersvelde Isaac
Dawn & Brent Jaeger
Christopher Jones
Carla Kelling
Meg Litts
Jim & Betty Ludden
Lynn Moorman

Jack & Jan Mutti
Cheryl Neubert
Martha Jane Pinder
Tina Popson & Corey McIntosh
Eleanor Osland
Sarah J. Purcell
The Rebelsky Family
Dick & Carolyn Ritter
Liz & Daniel Rodrigues
Mary Schuchmann
The Scruggs Family
Laura & Scott Shepherd
Sally & William Smith
Zane & Yefri Strawser-Picado
Valerie Vetter
Bob & Kim Wemer
Ted & Jane Williams
Alanna Walen

*And the 70 other individuals who offered financial support, and the many more who offered encouragement. Because of you the story of Edith Renfrow Smith can now be shared more easily.*

# No One Is Better Than You

# No One Is Better Than You

*Edith Renfrow Smith and the*
*Power of a Mother's Words*

Written by
**Monique McLay Shore**

Illustrations by
**Erica Lauren Butler**

First edition, January 2024
ISBN: 979-8-218-27050-6
Printed by Print Ninja

Second edition, July 2024
ISBN: 979-8-9909681-1-0
Printed by IngramSpark, a division of Ingram
*This edition marks the 110th birthday of Edith Renfrow Smith on July 14, 2024.*
*The last pages of this edition include a note from her to the author*
*as well as a photo of her holding the book.*

Scarlet Squirrel
Publishing

915 Summer St, Grinnell, IA 50112

To request permissions or for inquiries about prints of any illustrations,
contact the author at moniquemshore@gmail.com

For Edith, who waited 109 years for
someone to write her story.
I am grateful for her lessons, her love,
and the trust she placed in me.

**Edith Renfrow Smith** was **TENACIOUS** and **RESOLUTE.**

From the time she was little, until she was old and gray, she faced each day with **DETERMINATION,**

ready to greet each person with a **SMILE**

and each challenge with the **STRENGTH**

passed on from her family.

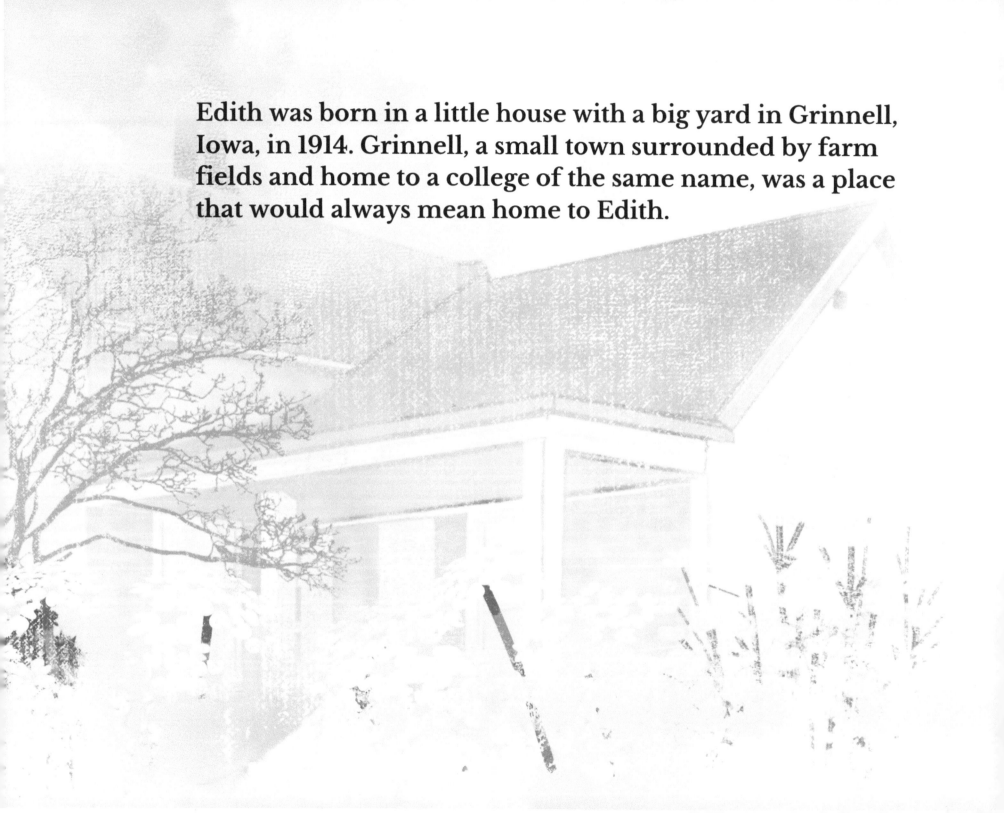

Edith was born in a little house with a big yard in Grinnell, Iowa, in 1914. Grinnell, a small town surrounded by farm fields and home to a college of the same name, was a place that would always mean home to Edith.

Edith had three older sisters - Helen, Alice, and Evanel - and one older brother, Rudy. She was six years younger than any of them. They were often away working when she was little. But when she was two, her little brother Paul was born. They were very close and did everything together—almost as if they were twins.

Being a Black family in a mostly white town made things difficult for the Renfrows. Edith's father, Lee, was a chef. He cooked at the town hotel and for special parties and sometimes took the train to other towns to find work. He would take any job he could find. At home, he had a giant garden where he grew corn, beans, carrots, parsnips-every kind of vegetable in the seed catalog. Edith and Paul helped by pulling weeds and picking vegetables. They especially loved to catch the garter snakes that slithered among the plants.

In the kitchen, Edith's mother, Eva Pearl, filled canning jars with tomatoes and peas, and packed the root cellar with potatoes and carrots to preserve them for the winter. Mama earned money by doing laundry for other people. She boiled the clothes in a big pot over a fire in the backyard, scrubbing them by hand on a washboard to get them clean. As often as she could, Mama would help with church and community events. She worked hard and made friends everywhere she went.

Edith's parents did all they could to support their family.
They made sure their children knew that they were loved
and that they could accomplish important things with their
lives. And every one of them would do just that.

Mama always told them,

"*No one* is better than you.

They may have more money.
They may be more beautiful.

But *no one* is *any better*
than *YOU*."

Little Edith loved to hear Mama share about their family and all they had overcome. "Mama, tell me a story," begged Edith.

Edith learned how her grandfather, George Craig, had escaped slavery in Missouri, traveling with others to freedom through Iowa. And how her grandmother, Eliza, had been born to an enslaved woman, and was sent away from her mother when she was only two years old.

She grew up free but never saw her mother again.

Edith never forgot
these stories.

When Edith was a young girl, Black men who were Grinnell College students often came to the Renfrow house for Sunday dinner. They were called Rosenwald Scholars. They sat around the table and told stories about their homes - places very different from Grinnell, like Chicago and Jamaica and Liberia.

After enjoying Mama's home cooked meal, everyone gathered around and sang while Edith's sisters played the piano. The men were smart and fun, and Edith loved being around them.

Edith also met college students at the youth club near her house, the Uncle Sam's Club. The college students taught them games and ran and jumped around with them. They were just like great big kids! But they also knew about science and new discoveries and inventions. They were so interesting! They made Edith curious about the world and want to explore new ideas. She wanted to go to Grinnell College to be like them.

Edith also loved being part of Camp Fire Girls. Her group leader, Laetitia Conard, did things that most women did not do at that time, like teaching at the college and driving a car. Once she took the girls on a camping trip several miles from town. Edith hadn't been on many car rides, and she had never been camping. She learned about nature and survival skills and the stars. It was all very exciting.

Mrs. Conard told the girls they could do anything boys could do. And she wanted children from poor families, like Edith's, to know that they were just as important as anyone else. Edith liked Mrs. Conard.

The things she said were just like what Mama always told her - that no one is any better than someone else because of how they look or where they live.

In high school, Edith did well in her classes and enjoyed all the activities, especially sports! She played basketball, volleyball, and field hockey.  She was always the only Black person on any of the teams.

Most people were nice to her, but there were some who were not.

In town, the candy store where kids liked to go wouldn't let her in because she was Black. And the movie theater would only let her sit in the worst seats in the balcony.

When people were mean like that, Edith remembered what Mama told her, "No one is any better than you". So she didn't let what people thought bother her, at least not very much.

After high school Edith was determined to go to Grinnell College, but she needed money to pay for it. Even if she lived at home, she still had to pay tuition - $275 dollars a year. That was a lot of money in the middle of the Great Depression in 1932. So Edith took classes to learn to type fast and take dictation. But even though she could type faster than anyone else in her class, no business in town would hire her.

So Edith looked for work at the
college. By the next fall she had
two jobs, one in the office of a
professor and the other working
in the copy center.

She was ready to become a
Grinnell College student.

Edith walked the mile to campus every day to go to classes, work, and spend time with the other students. She made friends and loved being a part of activities like dances and sports. She was even on the champion ring tennis team one year!

She met interesting people who came to teach and give talks, like Amelia Earhart, the first woman to fly a plane by herself across the Atlantic Ocean. After Earhart spoke to a big crowd in Herrick Chapel, she went to a gathering where she met with just the women students. Amelia Earhart just wanted to talk and laugh and have fun like the rest of them!

During the four years Edith attended Grinnell she was the only Black student on campus. There had been Black men at Grinnell before, like the Rosenwald Scholars who had visited her house when she was little. But there were never very many. Two Black women had gone to Grinnell before her, but neither of them had graduated.

So when Edith received her diploma in June 1937, she made history as the first Black woman to graduate from Grinnell College. It was a very happy day for Edith and her family. Mama asked a photographer to take Edith's picture so they would always remember that special day.

After graduation, Edith moved to Chicago and got a job. A few years later she met a nice man named Henry Smith. They got married in Grinnell in the living room of her parents' house, surrounded by all of the people and things that she loved.

As much as Edith liked Grinnell, she and Henry decided it would be better to raise their family in Chicago. Henry worked as a milkman and Edith was a secretary. They bought a house where they raised their two daughters, Virginia and Alice Frances.

In 1954, Edith decided to try something new. She took classes to become a 6th grade teacher. She loved working with children. She told her students,

"*No one* is better than you.

They may have more money.
They may be more beautiful.

But *no one* is *any better*
than *YOU*."

Many children had never heard anything like that before.
Edith gave them confidence and made them
believe in themselves.

After twenty-two years of teaching, Edith retired. But she still wanted to help people. So she volunteered - at Goodwill, the Chicago Art Institute, her church - anywhere she was needed. And she loved to drive! She volunteered to drive her friends around until she was well into her 90s.

She was an active volunteer for more than 40 years!

In 2009, when she was 95, she was inducted into the Chicago Senior Citizens Hall of Fame.

Chicago Senior Citizens
Hall of Fame 2009

Edith R. Smith,
Educator and Volunteer

Even though she lived in Chicago, Edith always thought of Grinnell as home. She and Henry visited as often as they could. Edith owned the house where she grew up until 2004 and rented it to other people, making sure it was a nice place to live.

When Edith and Henry visited Grinnell, they stayed with Alma and Booker Kiner, good friends who lived on a farm south of town. Edith and Alma cooked and baked treats, made soap, and talked and laughed together. Henry loved to help Booker do chores and work in the fields. When Edith and Henry went back to Chicago, Alma and Booker gave them fresh cream, eggs and other good things from the farm.

Edith never missed a Grinnell College reunion and the chance to visit with the friends she made when she was a student.

117

Smith Gallery
In honor of
Edith Renfrow Smith '37

At her 70th reunion in 2007, she was 93 years old. There weren't many people from her class left, but other alumni knew how important she was. So that year a student art gallery, the Smith Gallery, was named in her honor.

In 2019, when Edith was 104, Grinnell College awarded her an honorary Doctor of Humane Letters. It recognized her place in the history of the college and her life of giving to others.  It was May, but was a very cold day, so Edith wore a stocking cap to try to stay warm. The celebration of her life and accomplishments made her very proud and happy. The crowd gave her a standing ovation.

Edith went to the microphone and said,

# "Grinnell has been my life."

The more people heard about Edith, the more they wanted to know about her. Even though she was very old, she still had an incredibly sharp mind and quick wit.

In 2021, when she was 107, she came back to Grinnell for a special celebration and exhibit about her life in the Smith Gallery. She visited with students from the high school and from the college and shared her stories. She was the oldest person any of them had ever met.

Edith is always full of joy and positivity and a big smile.
She tells people what her mother told her,

"*No one* is better than you.

They may have more money.
They may be more beautiful.

But *no one* is *any better*
than *YOU*."

Talking with Edith makes people happy.
They want to be more like her.

In 2022, when Edith was 108, Grinnell College announced they were going to name a building after her. Renfrow Hall will be different from other college dorms, with both apartments for students and spaces for community events. Located between the campus and downtown, it will be a space to bring college people and community people together.

Edith Renfrow Smith is the oldest living graduate of both Grinnell High School and Grinnell College. She was born and raised in Grinnell. She is a part of the town history as well as the college history. She represents all that is good about both, and both will be celebrated in Renfrow Hall.

Renfrow Hall will open in 2024, 110 years after Edith was born in a little house with a big yard on First Avenue.

When Edith learned about Renfrow Hall she remembered all the things that she had lived through and all her memories of Grinnell. She thought about her mother and father and sisters and brothers. She knew they would be happy and proud that there would be a building in Grinnell with their family name on it.

She hoped that her story would help everyone
know that what her Mama had said was true.

That **IT DOESN'T MATTER** what you look like
or how much money you have.
It doesn't matter what other people think.

## BECAUSE NO ONE IS ANY BETTER THAN YOU.

If you focus on the good in others and in the world, and if you
are diligent and determined, you can overcome any obstacle.

You can **MAKE A DIFFERENCE**
and make the world a better place.

## YOU CAN BE LIKE EDITH.

# The Renfrow Story

Edith Renfrow Smith was born in Grinnell in 1914. She was raised in the community, attended Davis School through 6th grade and graduated from Grinnell High School in 1932. She became the first Black woman to graduate from Grinnell College in 1937. After graduation, she moved to Chicago where she met and married Henry Smith and raised her children, Virginia and Alice Frances. After working for several years at the University of Chicago, she returned to school and started a 22 year career as a 6th grade teacher. After retirement in 1976, she started to volunteer regularly at Goodwill and the Art Institute of Chicago, something she continued into her nineties. At the age of 94, she was inducted into the Chicago Senior Citizens Hall of Fame. Because of her remarkable vitality and memory, at the age of 99, Edith was selected to be a part of a "superager" study being conducted by Northwestern University.

In 2023, at age 109, Edith is the oldest living graduate of both Grinnell High School and Grinnell College. Throughout her life, she has lived by her mother's motto: "Nobody is better than you." Her life is a testament to the power of positivity and kindness and is an example all Grinnellians can embrace.

When Lee Augustus and Eva Pearl Craig Renfrow (parents of Edith Renfrow Smith) married in Grinnell in 1901, the roots of their families were already well established in Poweshiek County. They brought with them remarkable stories of escape from enslavement. Eva Pearl's parents, George and Eliza Jane Craig, had arrived in the community in the 1890s, having been in the Oskaloosa area since their marriage in 1862.

George Craig (grandfather of Edith) was born into slavery in Missouri. In order to save himself from being sold down South, he rubbed tobacco juice in his eyes to decrease his value on the auction block. At the age of 19, he escaped. He made his way to freedom via the Underground Railroad network, traveling through Grinnell with John Brown in 1859. This story was told by Mr. Craig and printed in the Grinnell Herald in March 1895.

Eliza Jane Craig (grandmother to Edith) was also born into slavery. Her mother was a slave named Jane. Her father was a French plantation owner, Antoine Gilbal, in South Carolina. Eliza was the third child from this relationship. Before his death, Gilbal sent the children north to freedom, making arrangements for them to be financially supported. Jane was to be freed at his death to follow the children, but his wishes were not honored and she remained enslaved, never to see her children again.

George and Eliza Craig had three daughters – Anna, Theodora and Eva Pearl. Each of the daughters would marry and live in Grinnell for a significant part of their lives. Theodora married John Brown Lucas in 1885; Anna married Ed Goode in 1887, was widowed, and later married Solomon Brown; and Eva Pearl married Lee Augustus Renfrow in 1901.

After their marriage, Lee and Eva Pearl Renfrow (parents to Edith Renfrow Smith) lived for a short time in Grinnell, where their first child, Helen, was born in 1904. By 1905 they had moved to Red Wing, MN, where they lived for a few years and where their next three children were born: Alice in 1906; Rudolph in 1907; and Evanel in 1908. By 1910 they had found their way back to Grinnell. Their return was encouraged by Mumford Holland, an elderly Black neighbor who asked Eva Pearl to help care for him during his final years of life. As payment, his home would become hers after his death. So it was that they moved to 511 Second Avenue, the home they inherited from Mumford, which was also next door to Eva Pearl's parents, George and Eliza Craig.

Lee Augustus Renfrow was primarily a cook, though he did whatever jobs he could find. He was employed at different establishments over the years, most notably at the Monroe Hotel, the preeminent lodging facility in Grinnell during that period. Eva Pearl was active in the community and in a variety of women's organizations at the time. They were members of the Congregational Church and she kept active raising her children and doing a variety of small jobs to help provide income. The family would often attend concerts and events on the Grinnell College campus, taking advantage of all that was available. Education was a high priority in the Renfrow household and missing school was never an option, according to Edith. After a few years on Second Avenue, they moved to 411 First Avenue. The Renfrow children walked to and from home to Davis School, and later to the Junior or Senior High at the corner of Fifth and Park, across from Central Park.

All of the Renfrow children knew it was expected that they would go to college. It was also a family understanding that they would work together to help support one another to achieve that goal. All of them worked in service jobs, there being few other positions open to Black people in Grinnell at the time. Their commitment to education and to one another enabled each of them to attend and complete college, then have successful careers.

The eldest, Helen (1904-1968), attended Fisk University and then the University of Iowa, where she later worked as a research technician in the internal medicine lab. She married Allyn Lemme and they became civil rights leaders in Iowa City. They helped support Black students at the University of Iowa during the time when Blacks were not allowed to live on campus. The Helen Lemme Elementary School in Iowa City is named in her honor, commemorating the impact she had on the community.

Alice Renfrow (1906-1997) attended Hampton University. In 1935 she accepted a position at the Library of Congress, where she worked for the next 40 years. She is buried with her parents and brothers in Hazelwood Cemetery.

Rudolph, Rudy to his family, Renfrow (1907-1972) attended Hampton and graduated valedictorian of his class. He settled in the D.C. area where he was employed in sales and engaged in civil rights work, including as part of the New Negro Alliance in the 1930s. He is also buried in Hazelwood Cemetery with his parents and sister.

Evanel Renfrow Terrell (1909-1994) received both a Bachelor's and Master's degree from the University of Iowa. She went on to a career as a Professor of Home Economics in African American universities across the south, culminating in a 27-year tenure at Savannah State University. She was married to Carl Terrell.

Paul Renfrow (1917-1974) attended school in Chicago. When WW II broke out, he enlisted in the US Army. He was a part of the D-Day invasion and reached the rank of Master Sergeant before his discharge. He became an optician and practiced in Washington, D.C. for most of his life. He is also buried at Hazelwood Cemetery.

George and Eliza Craig family 1902. Eva Pearl Craig is at center of the back row.

Edith Renfrow, age 2

Edith Renfrow 8th grade

Edith and her mother

Eva Pearl Craig Renfrow in her wedding gown.

Paul (left) and Edith (center back) with cousins Mercedes and Virginia Mays.

Edith Renfrow Grinnell College graduation 1937

Mother Edith with her oldest daughter Virginia and a niece, Elsie (standing)

The Renfrow Sisters - Evanel, Edith, Alice and Helen

Rudy

Paul

Each of the Renfrow children had impressive lives.
Helen was an Iowa City leader (Helen Lemme
Elementary School is named in her honor).
Alice worked for the Library of Congress of 40 years.
Evanel was a Professor of Home Economics.
Rudy was a civil rights leader in Washington DC and
Paul was an optician, also in DC.

Edith's daughter, Alice, with neighbor Herbie Hancock.
Mr. Hancock would later attend Grinnell College
with Edith's encouragement. He was one of
many individuals who attended Grinnell
because of her influence.

Mrs. Edith Smith, Chicago teacher, sometime
in the 1950s.

Edith in front of the Chicago Institute of Art, as
featured on the Grinnell Magazine cover in
2007.

Edith and Henry Smith celebrating their
50th anniversary.

For her 100th birthday, Edith bought herself this little red
Fiat. She continued to drive for a couple more years.

All photos are from the Renfrow Family Collection, courtesy of Drake Community Library
(Grinnell, Iowa), or the personal collection of the author, unless otherwise noted.

In 2015, at age 101, Edith returned to Grinnell. She was interviewed by Dan Kaiser at Drake Community Library.

Receiving Doctor of Humane Letters from Grinnell College in 2019. (Image courtesy of Grinnell College)

Professor Tamara Beauboeuf, Edith, and Feven Getachew celebrate the rededication of the Smith Gallery in October 2021. (Photo credit Justin Hayworth, Grinnell College)

Monique Shore, Edith, and Dan Kaiser at a celebratory dinner in October 2021.

The day President Harris told Edith about the naming of Renfrow Hall.
Myrna Hernandez, Anne Harris, and Monique Shore with Edith in Chicago, October 2022.

April 2023, age 108, at a friends and family celebration in Chicago for the naming of Renfrow Hall.
(Photo courtesy of Justin Hayworth, Grinnell College)

Monique Shore, Alice Smith, Tamara Beaubouef and Edith, celebrating her 109th birthday in July 2023.

Edith with the summer 2023 Team Renfrow research group.
Left to right, Hemlock Stanier, Evie Caperton, Tamara Beauboeuf, Edith, Monique Shore, and Libby Eggert.

# My Edith Story
by Monique McLay Shore

I first met Edith Renfrow Smith when she was a spry 101 year old. She came to Drake Community Library in Grinnell, Iowa, along with her daughter, Alice, in 2015. They arrived with several dozen family photos to scan for the library's digital archive project that I manage, and to do a live oral history interview. Dan Kaiser, retired Grinnell College history professor, who had started researching her family a few years earlier, conducted the interview. His research was the impetus for reaching out to Edith. After that visit I received a package of homemade fudge and a lovely handwritten note. It would be the first of many such gifts. Little did I know how that first meeting would evolve into something much bigger.

The next time I saw Edith was in 2019 when she received an honorary degree from Grinnell College. We had dinner together. She was moving a bit slower, but was still simply remarkable. It was wonderful to see her receive this honor from our alma mater and, since she was nearly 105, it seemed probable that this might be our last encounter. But the best was yet to come.

In the summer of 2021, just as the world was starting to reopen after the pandemic, a young woman walked into Drake Community Library and asked if we had anything about Edith Renfrow Smith in our archives. I still remember the moment I first set eyes on Feven Getachew and, with a big smile, offered her the box of materials we had accumulated. A few days later she returned with Grinnell College Professor Tamara Beauboeuf. When they said they'd love to meet Edith I was thrilled to be able to put them in touch. Their summer of research included two visits to Chicago and culminated in Edith and Alice again visiting Grinnell that fall. The rededication of the Edith Renfrow Smith Gallery on campus was a wonderful celebration of Edith and her life. The small group who had helped make it happen gathered for a joyous meal at Prairie Canary that night to celebrate together.

The summer of 2022 included another Team Renfrow visit to Chicago and things continued to evolve. We learned more about the reach of her family story into the early history of Grinnell and were able to meet with Grinnell College President, Anne Harris, to share what we had learned. Her decision to pursue naming the newest college building Renfrow Hall in Edith's honor was the culmination of our shared dream. It was an incredible honor to be able to be a part of the meeting when President Harris shared this news with Edith.

In the midst of all of this, with some gentle nudging and encouragement from Tamara, the idea of writing this book was hatched.

After spending so much time hearing Edith share about her family and experiences, I had a pretty good grasp on the key points of her story. I wasn't too worried about what to write. But I had no idea how to get it illustrated. Given the Grinnell focus of the story, I reached out to the online alumni community for ideas. Through this network I connected with illustrator, Erica L. Butler. After seeing samples of her work and an initial conversation, I felt confident I had found someone who could help bring this vision to life.

With that piece in place, the next step was to talk to Edith. I made a booklet with the text I had drafted and headed to Chicago in March 2023. We sat next to each other and she carefully followed along in her copy as I read the words to her and Alice for the first time. I was overjoyed by her response and thrilled when she offered affirmation by saying, "you were the one who was meant to do it." In that moment, more than any before, I knew I had been entrusted to carry and deliver an incredible treasure. My promise to her, to Alice, and to myself, was that I would honor the trust they had placed in me and would do everything I could to ensure this book was something that would bring joy and carry her story into the future.

The next step was to figure out how to pay Erica for creating the illustrations. I launched a Kickstarter campaign in April with the goal of raising $10,000 to cover the illustrations and initial print expenses. The support from the Grinnell community members and college alumni was overwhelming and the campaign goal was met in only four days! Erica and I began talking regularly. I shared photos and videos of Edith and Grinnell she could use for reference. In the meantime, the college alumni office had put me in touch with Caroline Arnold. The author of more than 100 children's books, she provided wonderful guidance and editing advice.

Edith and Alice were involved every step of the way. Some early illustrations included things that they said weren't right: hair was too thick and clothes were too fancy; her father was always off working and was seldom around, so he shouldn't be in any pictures; and public affection like parents holding hands, that we thought conveyed a loving family, had to go because it would not have been acceptable at that time. Edith had a loving family, it was just a different world a hundred years ago, so the illustrations needed to reflect that. All of this added extra time and expense for the illustrations, but it was worth it to create a book that would honor and respect the life we were depicting. The pictures may not be perfect in every detail, but we've done our best and hope they capture the essence of the story and make it engaging to readers.

I documented each step of the process on the book website **renfrowstory.com** so others could follow the progress. Long term, I will contribute materials related to the book process to the archives of Drake Community Library so it can be included with the other Renfrow materials.

*Reading the story to Edith and Alice for the first time.*
*(March 2023)*

# A Note from Alice Frances Smith
## Daughter of Edith Renfrow Smith

My family and friends have long wished for a story that honors my mother's character, legacy and life. Working to bring her story to fruition has brought back many rich memories, lively stories and questions about the intimate parts of her life. The words of the author have brought delight to both my mother and me as we have seen the story develop. While working on each detail has not been without its challenges, this is also part of the challenges faced in life. My mother is humble, gracious and gifted with praise for others and their work. Through the process, my family and I have marveled at the conversations, engagement and willingness of the author to reflect with us on the messages sent. I am thankful for their willingness to bring my mother's story to life for generations yet to come.

*Alice Frances Smith*

## About the Author

*Monique and Edith, May 2019.*

Monique McLay Shore was born and raised in southern Nevada. When she attended Grinnell College she fell in love with the community. She has worked at the public library in Grinnell since 1991 and has overseen the technology evolution in library services for the last 30 years. Active in the community and as a college volunteer, she thoroughly enjoys learning and sharing Grinnell history with others.

Not counting small projects for family and friends, this is her first book.

## About the Artist

*Erica L. Butler*

Seattle-based illustrator Erica Lauren Butler (Raven to her friends), has been making waves in the art world with her stunning and unique creations. Her work is a beautiful blend of traditional and modern styles, with a focus on bold colors and intricate details. Erica draws inspiration from nature, mythology, and her own personal experiences, resulting in pieces that are both visually striking and deeply meaningful.

In addition to her work as an illustrator, Erica is also passionate about giving back to her community.

*"I've been honored to illustrate the story of Mrs. Edith Renfrow Smith. It's s dream job, partly because her story reflects the experience of many Black families, including my own."*

To contact the artist, email golanv1@yahoo.com
Or visit her on Facebook: https://www.facebook.com/erica.branchbutler

Left: Edith Renfrow Smith holds the first copy of this book on December 2, 2023.

Below: A note written by Edith Renfrow Smith on May 30, 2024 to the author.

This note was written by Edith on May 30, 2024. It was about six weeks before her 110th birthday and about six months after the first copies were received.

Though her handwriting is shaky and a few words are jumbled, I believe this is what it says:

May 30, 2024

Dear Monique, such a talented author.
 Who would have thought in a million years that those daily admonitions would give someone the ability to make something so delightful. It seems anyone who touches it delights and wishes to open and see what it holds, adults and children. And it means so much to the college and my family.
 Please thank Anne for me.

Sincerely, Edith

I think the last bit about thanking Anne must mean Grinnell College President Anne Harris, who was the champion for the naming of Renfrow Hall.

This treasured note will be kept with the photo of her holding a copy of the book for the first time.

## My Thanks and Gratitude To These People

I am especially grateful to the incomparable Mrs. Edith Renfrow Smith for her love and encouragement. And to her daughter, Alice, for the many hours of feedback she provided to make this a more true reflection of the life of her mother.

Many thanks to Grinnell College President Anne Harris and her leadership team for their encouragement and support, especially to Cassie Wherry and the staff at the Pioneer Bookstore.

Editorial assistance from fellow alumna Caroline Arnold made this a much better book and is very much appreciated.

To Erica, who spent many, many hours perfecting the illustrations. This was a labor of love that became overwhelming at times. I am grateful for the time and energy she gave to going above and beyond what I could pay her. Her work is beautiful and I encourage anyone looking for an illustrator to connect with her.

Special thanks to Dan, Tamara, and Feven, the original Team Edith, for all they did to help bring the story of this remarkable woman to light. It has been wonderful to be on this journey of discovery and enlightenment together.

And above all, I couldn't have done this without the support of my entire family. I am especially grateful to my husband, Craig, for his endless patience, support and belief in me and the things I get myself into. And to our daughter, Moraine. My life is complete because of you two.

Printed in the USA
CPSIA information can be obtained
at www.ICGtesting.com
CBHW041203190724

11673CB00004B/36